Artists' Workshop

Sports
and Games

Penny King and Clare Roundhill

Crabtree Publishing Company

Crabtree Publishing Company

350 Fifth Avenue	360 York Road, R.R.4	73 Lime Walk
Suite 3308	Niagara-on-the-Lake	Headington, Oxford
New York, NY 10118	Ontario L0S 1J0	England OX3 7AD

Edited by **Bobbie Kalman**
Assistant Editor **Virginia Mainprize**
Designed by **Mei Lim**
Illustrations by **Lindy Norton**

Children's pictures by
**Emily Ashworth, Amy Browne, Lucy Caminada, Emma Carrington-Brook,
Amber Civardi, Louise Cramsie, Charlotte Downham, Lucy Figgis, Louisa Fisher,
Purdey Fitzherbert, James Jarman, Sophie Lewis, Alice Masson-Taylor, Georgie Mew,
Lottie Mew, Archie Parrack, Sam Pepper, Flora Pethybridge, Susie Roberts,
Georgina Smith, Thomas Stofer, Florence Turner, Jessica Williams**
Picture research by **Sara Elliott**
Photographs by **Steve Shott**

Created by
Anne Civardi
Copyright © 1997 Anne Civardi

Cataloging-in-Publication Data

King, Penny, 1963-
Sports and games/Penny King and Clare Roundhill
p.   cm. - (Artists' Workshop)
Includes index.
Summary: Presents six works of art with sports themes to be used as starting points for exploring
various artistic techniques. Includes instructions and examples for creating one's own work.
ISBN 0-86505-864-4 (paper). – ISBN 0-86505-854-7 (RHB)
1. Child artists - Psychology - Juvenile literature. 2. Sports in art - Juvenile literature.
3. Games in art - Juvenile literature. [1. Art - Technique. 2. Sports in art.]
I. Roundhill, Clare, 1964-   . II. Title. III Series: King, Penny. 1963- Artists' workshops.
N351.K5   1997   704'.054-DC21   97-24692
                                                                CIP
                                                                AC

First published in 1997 by
A & C Black (Publishers) Limited
35 Bedford Row, London WC1R 4JH

Printed in Hong Kong by Wing King Tong Co Ltd

Cover photograph: **Henri Rousseau** The Football Players (Les Joueurs de football) 1908
Oil on canvas 100.5 x 80.3 cm (39 1/2 x 31 5/8 inches); Solomon R. Guggenheim Museum, New York
Henri Rousseau was a French artist who taught himself to paint by copying famous pictures.
He is best known for his large, decorative pictures of people and animals set in extraordinary
or dreamlike settings which he painted in strong, bright colors.

Contents

The sporting scene

For thousands of years, sports and games have played an important part in people's lives. Over the centuries, artists have pictured sports events and athletes on cave walls, frescoes, vases, stamps and coins, as well as in paintings.

In Roman times, gladiator fights were very popular. Watched by blood-thirsty crowds, the gladiators fought to the death against wild animals and other gladiators.

The Olympic Games, which began over 2,000 years ago, gave athletes the chance to show off their agility and strength in front of huge crowds. Many of the events, such as running, javelin-throwing and wrestling, were also part of a soldier's training for war.

Today, people can watch all kinds of sports on television, or in stadiums which hold thousands of spectators. Many of the players earn a lot of money and have become sports heroes in games such as soccer, tennis and baseball.

For the spectators, the contests were exciting shows of strength and bravery. For the athletes, training and skill could mean the difference between life and death.

In this book, there are six works of art showing people taking part in different sports and games. Three of the pieces are very old and three are more modern. The artists have not only shown the event, but have also captured its mood, from the silent concentration of a checkers game to the noisy activity of a busy playground.

Think about the sports and games you enjoy and then use the artists' ideas to create your own sporting pictures. Imagine yourself either as one of the players or as a spectator at an important game. You may want to make some sketches before you start.

Try to show the feelings of the players and the excitement of the crowds. Think about the colors you could use and the best way to show activity and movement, light and shadow. You could frame your pictures and give them as presents to your family and friends.

Greek games

These two ancient Greek soldiers are playing a game of checkers. The picture is painted on an amphora, a vase used for storing wine or food. A famous Greek potter and painter, named Exekias, made it over 2,500 years ago.

Signed by Exekias *Achilles and Ajax Playing Checkers c.600 BC. Photo Vatican Museums*

The picture shows Achilles and Ajax, two mythical Greek heroes, relaxing between battles during the Trojan War. These two brave and strong soldiers are in full armor, holding their spears, ready to spring into action.

Most people and animals in ancient Greek art are shown from the side. The black figures, which stand out against the red clay background, are called silhouettes. Vases decorated in this way often tell stories of Greek myths.

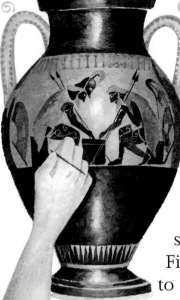

Exekias shaped the vase on a potter's wheel. It was made from reddish brown clay dug from the ground. First, he painted the black silhouettes and then scratched out the details with a sharp needle. The red clay shines through the black paint. Finally, the pot was fired in a kiln to harden the clay.

In those days, athletes were admired for their grace, skill and strength. Many vases were decorated with pictures of strong, young men competing against each other. Exekias was one of the first Greek artists to paint people in a realistic way. Look at their powerful arms and legs!

Greek pots of all shapes and sizes are known as vases. Some were used to transport food to other countries. They have been found many miles away from Greece. Thousands of these ancient vases have survived because clay is so strong. Also, people did not think them valuable enough to steal.

Greek profiles

People today admire athletes, just as the ancient Greeks did. Imagine yourself a Greek artist and create your own silhouettes of sports heroes.

You could pretend that you have been watching the ancient Olympic Games and are recording an exciting victory which has just taken place.

Scratchy sportsmen

Cover a piece of white cardboard with a thick layer of brightly colored wax crayon. Using thick, black poster paint, paint a border and a picture of an athlete on top of the wax. When the paint is almost dry, use a knitting needle to scratch out the face and other details. The wax crayon will shine through just as Exekias's patterns did on his vase.

Clay vase

Make a simple vase out of self-hardening clay or a modeling material such as DAS. Roll out some clay for the handles. Wet the ends and press them onto the sides of the vase. When the clay is hard, paint it a bright color. With a pencil, draw the outline of a runner and then fill it in with black paint. Use a gold pen to decorate the figure.

Paper silhouettes

Choose two pieces of colored construction paper that contrast well with each other, such as yellow and black. On one piece, draw a large vase and cut it out. On the other piece, draw the silhouette of an athlete throwing a javelin. Carefully cut out the picture and glue it onto the vase. Use the rest of the paper to make a repeating pattern to decorate the rim and base of the vase.

Magnificent marbles

Use bold shapes and bright colors to create pictures with a Roman feel. By painting one side of a flat sponge and printing with it, you can give your paper a marbled effect.

Racing colors

On white paper, draw the outline of a jockey's face and shirt. Crumple a piece of skin-colored tissue paper and then flatten it out again. Glue it over the jockey's face, allowing it to go over the outline. With another color tissue paper do the same thing for the shirt.

Cut out the jockey, trimming off the extra tissue paper. Cut shapes from brightly colored paper for his eyes, nose, mouth and hair, as well as the decorations on his shirt. Glue them onto the jockey. Then glue your picture onto a colored background.

Jigsaw horse

Paint one side of a flat sponge with a dark colored paint, such as deep blue. Press the sponge, paint side down, all over a sheet of white paper. When the paint is dry, sponge paler blue over the top. Sponge another piece of paper in a different color, such as red.

Draw a big prancing horse, or a horse's head and shoulders, on the back of one sheet and cut it out. Cut the horse into pieces, as shown. Arrange them on the second sheet of paper and glue them in place, leaving small gaps in between.

Handsome horses

Draw the outline of a horse on stiff cardboard and cut it out. This is your outline model or template. Fold a sheet of colored paper in half. Draw around your template to create a group of horses on the left side. Make sure they all face in the same direction. Flip the template over and draw another group of horses facing the other way. Paint the horses different colors.

Children's games

Here is a picture full of action and noise.
It was painted in oils on a big wooden panel over
400 years ago. The artist, Pieter Bruegel, has shown
children playing over eighty different games.
How many can you see?

Pieter Bruegel the Elder *Children's Games* 1560. Kunsthistorisches Muesum, *Vienna*

Bruegel is famous for pictures crowded with people. In many of his paintings, such as this one, he shows how people can change a quiet landscape. Here, hundreds of children have taken over the town square, the road, the buildings and even the peaceful park.

Every single child is busy. Some are playing leapfrog and tug-of-war. Others prefer games with toys such as hobby horses and spinning tops. A few are pretending to be adults in a marriage ceremony and a tournament. Can you see some boys being picked on by playground bullies?

The artist loved to show people in action. In fact, he rarely painted still figures unless it was to show that they were lazy, asleep or dead! He studied the shapes that people's bodies make as they move and then worked on painting their outlines. He spent less time on the details of their faces and clothes.

Bruegel has painted the scene as if he were standing high above the ground, almost from a bird's-eye view. He has filled the picture with contrasting colors. Look at how the children painted red show up far more than those painted in shades of blue and brown.

You feel as if you could almost walk into the picture and join in the games. This feeling is created by perspective. The figures at the front are larger than those in the middle. As they disappear down the road they become tiny dots. The road becomes narrower as it goes further away until it, too, is just a speck.

Playtime pranks

Watch your friends as they play. When they move, notice what happens to their hair and clothes as well as their arms, head and legs.

Look at a crowd of people. Some people are close together in groups, others are further apart. When you create your Bruegel picture, remember how the crowd looked.

Motion pictures

Sketch pictures of your friends in different positions. What happens when they spin around? Do their clothes and hair fan out? Look at the way people's arms and legs bend when they run, skip and hop. Paint a picture based on the sketch you like best.

Dressing up

Create a felt collage of some of the children in Bruegel's painting. You may want to use lots of red and blue as Bruegel did in his picture.

Draw the shapes you need on the back of pieces of colored felt with a pencil or wax crayon. Like Bruegel, concentrate on the shapes of clothes and bodies rather than the children's faces. Cut the shapes out and arrange them on colored construction paper. Use strong glue to stick them on the paper, drawing side down.

Creating crowds

To create a crowd that looks real, draw lots of children on pieces of white paper. Draw large ones for the foreground, medium-sized ones for the middle and small ones for the background. Color them with felt-tipped pens and cut them out. Arrange the pictures on a sheet of paper and glue them in overlapping groups, starting with the figures in the background.

Show of strength

This beautifully detailed picture comes from a book of Persian stories, each of which has its own moral. The book was given as a present to the man sitting on the throne, Akbar, the Mogul Emperor of India.

From the Gulistan of Sa'di Persian (Bukara) 1567. British Library, London

The picture tells the story of a wise wrestler who knew 360 cunning tricks. He kept one a secret from his pupils. During a contest before the king, a pupil tried to beat this wrestler.

After a long, hard fight, the young man was defeated by the wise wrestler's secret hold. The moral of this story is that a secret plan may one day protect you from an enemy.

Persian painters made their own paintbrushes from hairs of the fluffy tails of furry animals. The artists tied hairs of exactly the same length together in different-sized bundles. They made very thin bundles for fine brush strokes and thicker bundles for bolder strokes.

The artist, Shahm Muzahhib, painted all the people in the picture the same size. Most European artists would have painted the people in the foreground bigger than those further away. (Think back to the painting by Bruegel.)

So he wouldn't make a mistake, Muzahhib first drew his design on rough paper. He put a transparent sheet of deerskin over it and pricked out the outline of the design with a needle. Then he placed the pin-pricked deerskin over another sheet of paper.

He dusted powdered charcoal over the pinpricks, leaving an outline of black dots on the paper below. Finally, he joined up the dots and carefully filled in all the details.

Powerful Persians

At sports events, the people watching seem to enjoy themselves just as much as the players. Look at the excited spectators in Muzahhib's picture.

You can create your own picture of a strong athlete or an excited spectator dressed in fine clothes. You could also design a beautifully patterned rug like the Persian rugs in the painting on page 18.

Join the Dots

Draw the outline of a weightlifter on a piece of paper. With the point of a sharp pencil, prick holes around the outline. Place the picture on top of a sheet of the same sized paper. Clip the sheets together.

Pressing firmly, color over the holes with a felt-tipped pen. Join the dots together on the paper below. Color in the weightlifter's clothes and face.

Dressed-up spectators

Draw the outline of a spectator on white paper. Paint in the face, hands and feet. While the paint is drying, cut out shapes from patterned wrapping paper or old magazine pictures. Stick the pieces closely together to create colorful clothes and a beautiful turban.

Sporty rugs

Design a Persian-style rug for a sports club. Using a ruler, draw a rectangle in the middle of a sheet of white paper. Draw two or three larger rectangles around it to create frames. Fill the frames with drawings of sports equipment such as a tennis racket or a soccer ball. Draw a larger picture in the middle. Color the rug with felt-tipped pens.

Smooth sailing

As a boy, Edward Hopper sketched the boats on the Hudson River near his home in Nyack, New York. He loved sailing, and at fifteen he built his own boat. His understanding of how boats work helps make this picture look very real.

Edward Hopper The Long Leg 1935. © Virginia Steele Scott Foundation, The Huntington Library and Art Gallery, San Marino, California

Many of Hopper's paintings have a feeling of loneliness. Here the lighthouse seems tiny and lost compared to the huge, open sky and the flat, blue sea. The picture is full of opposites: light and shade, land and water, pale and dark colors.

Using shades of blue oil paint, Hopper captured the feeling of a clear, breezy morning. He was fascinated by the way light changes at different times of day. In this picture, the sun is shining onto the side of the lighthouse and the sails of the boat skimming over the water.

Hopper liked to use oil paints. These are made by mixing a little powdered color into linseed, walnut or poppy oil. Oil paints can be made into rich, thick colors or thin, transparent ones. Although it dries slowly, the paint stays just as bright when it is dry as when it was wet.

The artist thought that people in big cities like New York felt lonely and unimportant. In many of his pictures, he shows people all alone in dark, dingy places, such as cafés or railway stations. Even those who are shown sitting next to each other are not talking. They seem lost in their own private thoughts.

Unlike many artists, Hopper was not interested in painting flowers and animals, the changing seasons or the weather. He preferred to paint simple, uncluttered pictures. He once said that it took him years before he could even bring himself to paint a cloud.

Away from it all

Use poster paints to paint a picture of a sport you would like to do alone or with a friend. You can make poster paint thick and shiny by mixing it with glue and flour. Use shades of one color, just as Hopper did in his sailing picture.

Think about the colors that go well with the sport, such as blue for watersports and green for golf or games you play on the grass.

Stormy sailing

Imagine how Hopper would have painted the sailboat and the sea in the middle of a storm. Mix shades of icy blue for the sea and gray for the sky. Use streaks and dashes of white for the foamy waves and falling rain. Add a lighthouse flashing to warn passing ships and boats.

Flying high

Mix blue and yellow paint together to make green. Create other shades of green by adding extra blue or yellow. To make the colors paler, add a little white.

Use these colors to paint a Hopper-style landscape of rolling hills, trees and bushes. When it is dry, paint in a small child flying a colorful kite high in the sky.

Lonely beaches

Crumple up some pieces of blue and yellow tissue paper and then flatten them out again to give an uneven texture. Cover a piece of white paper with glue. Stick down the blue tissue for the sea and the sky and yellow tissue for the sand. Tear up pieces of brightly colored paper for a sailboat and a lighthouse.

Splash!

Leon Kossoff became fascinated by this noisy swimming pool while he was teaching his son how to swim. Before he painted this picture, he spent months watching how the light changed during the day, in every kind of weather and at different times of the year.

Leon Kossoff Children's Swimming Pool, 11 o'clock Saturday Morning, August 1969. Private collection

This huge painting, filled with light, space and movement, is over 6½ feet (two meters) wide and 5 feet (1.5 meters) tall. Kossoff shows the August sun as it pours through the windows and shines on the tiled floor.

Even though he has not shown the children in great detail, we can still imagine what they are doing. Many seem to be bursting with energy. They dive into the water, swim and play. Others are standing at the poolside, ready to jump.

Kossoff has used all kinds of wavy, straight and curved lines. This gives the picture a feeling of busy movement. The way he has dabbed on thick streaks and dashes of oil paint in every direction makes the scene look even busier.

Before he painted the pool, the artist drew many sketches of it to help him remember the noise, steamy warmth and excitement. He did not take any photographs, as other artists might have, to remind him of what was happening. Kossoff believes that photographs lose all the feeling of the moment.

Leon Kossoff Children's Swimming Pool No. 2, 1972. © Leon Kossoff

Kossoff has used cool blues for the water and chilly grays and whites for the building. By painting the children in warm reds and oranges, he has made them look happy and full of energy. At the shallow end of the pool, a spray of white paint shows the water splashing over the sides.

Waterworld

Next time you go to a crowded swimming pool, listen to the children shrieking and splashing in the water. Look at what the children are doing, as they play, dive and swim, or just shiver by the poolside. Notice how smooth the water is when nobody is in the pool compared to when it is full of swimmers.

Splashing swimmers

Use a pencil or a fine black felt-tipped pen to make sketches of children playing in a swimming pool. Choose the sketches you like best to create a painting.

Lightly sketch the figures on white paper and paint them in warm colors. Mix lots of shades of thick, blue paint. Using a wide brush, paint wavy water all around the swimmers.

Daring divers

On watercolor paper, draw a simple outline of a person diving into the water. Mix several shades of thin blue paint. Wet the paper with a wide paintbrush. Quickly paint dashes and streaks of blue all over the background. Paint the diver's body and swimsuit as well with watery paints. Don't worry if the paint goes over the outline, as this gives the effect of water splashing over the diver.

Making waves

Mix several shades of blue paint. To show calm water, paint wide streaks of blue across a white background. For rough water, paint different-sized triangles of blue. When the paint is dry, cover it with a thick layer of glue.

Cut blue wool into different lengths and press them into the glue. Long, slightly wavy lines look calm; wiggly, messy ones look wild and rough. You might like to add pink paper feet sticking out of the water!

29

More about the artists and pictures

Exekias
(Greek)
Achilles and Ajax Playing Checkers c.600 BC

Exekias lived and worked in the ancient Greek city of Athens and is considered the best potter and painter of his time. He was one of the first artists to paint humans rather than animals on vases. All the people in his pictures, from humble slaves to mighty gods, are painted with the same care and attention. Exekias filled his vases with detail. He was also one of the first painters to sign his works of art.

Roman Marble Artists
Chariot Race c.330-350 AD

It took many years for a marble artist to learn his trade. As a young boy, he worked as an apprentice to a master artist, learning how to cut and polish marble, mix cement and lay the slabs. He watched the master fill in the fine details. Once the apprentice had learned how to use all the tools, he would be allowed to design and create his own pictures. Then he, too, became a master artist.

Pieter Bruegel the Elder
(active 1550/1 - died 1569   Flemish)
Children's Games 1560

Named after the place where he was born, Pieter Bruegel the Elder was one of the first artists to paint landscapes. Many of his early pictures were crammed with tiny, busy figures. Later, his scenes became far less crowded. Among his most famous paintings are twelve pictures, each illustrating one of the twelve months of the year. Bruegel traveled through Europe where he was inspired by the mountains of Italy, which appear in many of his paintings.

Shahm Muzahhib
(Persian)
Wrestling c.1567

In the days of the Persian Empire, beautifully illustrated books were greatly treasured by the royal family and nobles of the court. A royal court, presided over by a noble ruler, often had its own workshop which produced these expensive books. Here, scribes wrote down the words on carefully drawn lines, while artists painted the beautifully detailed pictures. Some of the pages were even sprinkled with gold dust.

Edward Hopper
(1882 - 1967   American)
The Long Leg 1935

From the age of seven, when he used his blackboard as an easel, Hopper wanted to be a painter. For twenty-five years, he illustrated shopping catalogs and advertisements. Hopper hated this job and lived cheaply so that he could spend all his money on art materials and painting trips. As soon as people began to buy his pictures, Hopper became a full-time artist.

Leon Kossoff
(Born 1926   English)
Children's Swimming Pool 1969

Leon Kossoff has always lived and worked in London. At the age of thirteen, when he moved to the countryside during the Second World War, he began drawing and painting the scenery around him. After the war, he went to art school. Kossoff likes to show the effect that light and the different seasons have on city life. He often paints crowded pictures that show how the busy people of London live, pouring in and out of subway or railway stations.

Other things to do

1 To make your own sports collage, paint a piece of cardboard, either with green dashes to look like a grassy field or bold stripes for team colors. When the paint is dry, glue on any sporting souvenirs you have collected, such as magazine pictures, tickets, programs or photographs of your favorite sports heroes.

2 Roman athletes were given a laurel wreath when they won a sports event. Cut two strips of green construction paper about 1 inch (2.5 cm) wide. Glue the strips together so they will fit around your head. Cut out leaves and glue them along the strip. Now you have your own laurel wreath.

3 Use water-soluble crayons to draw a picture of a racing car speeding around a track. Dampen a flat sponge and drag it over the picture, from the front of the car to the back and a little beyond. You will see that the colors blur, giving the feeling of speed.

4 To make an Olympic torch, cut out a large cardboard circle. Cut a hole in the middle the same size as the end of a paper towel tube. Push the cardboard onto the tube, as shown. Paint the tube and cardboard gold. Fold single sheets of red, yellow, orange, pink and blue tissue paper in half. Lay them on top of each other. Twist one set of ends together and push them into one end of the paper towel tube. Tear or cut the tissue so that it looks like flickering flames.

Index

Acknowledgements

The publishers are grateful to the following institutes and individuals for permissionto reproduce the illustrations on the pages mentioned.
Photograph by David Heald c The Solomon R. Guggenheim Foundation, New York FN60.1583: cover; Vatican Museum, Rome: 6; SCALA Instituto Fotografico Editoriale, Florence: 10; Kunsthistorisches Museum, Vienna: 14; Persian 1567 Or. 5302 (Fol. 30a), by permission of The British Library: 18; SuperStock Ltd: 22; James D. Edmundson Fund, Des Moines Art Center, Iowa: 23; Private collection: 26; Arts Council Collection, Hayward Gallery: 27.